T0132295

ZOO
BASEBALL

Written by **Michael D. Dwyer**
Illustrated by **Nancy D. Herlihy**

AuthorHouse™
1663 Liberty Drive
Bloomington, IN 47403
www.authorhouse.com
Phone: 1 (800) 839-8640

Published by AuthorHouse 02/14/2019

ISBN: 978-1-7283-0066-5 (sc)
ISBN: 978-1-7283-0065-8 (e)
ISBN: 978-1-7283-0091-7 (hb)

Library of Congress Control Number: 2019901848

author**HOUSE**®

Zoo Baseball

Danny stretched awake and smiled thinking about the day ahead of him. Today he was going to the zoo with his dad. Tomorrow he had his first baseball practice.

He put on his new baseball jersey and hat and headed down the stairs.
After breakfast, dad grabbed their lunches and they headed out the door.

As they entered the zoo Danny asked, "How will I know what to do at baseball?" "I have an idea," his dad replied, "let's let the animals help you."

Walking around the corner, they spied the alligator sunning herself, mouth wide open. "Look, she looks as if she is ready to catch a ground ball," said dad. "Just like the alligator's mouth, you need to keep your mitt down and your other hand above it to help the ball stay in your glove."

A little further down the path, Danny saw a lion crouched down, intently watching something in the grass. "See how the lion stays low to the ground? In baseball, when the batter is at home plate, fielders should be ready to pounce on the ball if it comes their way," said Danny's dad. "Gee dad, I bet the lion would make a great fielder, but he might eat the ball instead of throwing it to his teammates!" They both laughed and kept walking.

The building also housed some small reptiles. The lizard, with his long sticky tongue, was Danny's favorite. How great it would be to catch a baseball as quickly as the lizard caught flies.

Dad said an important part of baseball was hitting the ball. "Look at the elephant. He could use his trunk as a baseball bat and hit the ball far." Dad reminded him that he needed to keep his hands together and use his arms to swing. Above all, he told Danny that hitting takes patience and lots of practice.

Dad continued, "After you hit the ball, you need to run to first base. If you hit it, and no one catches it, you can try to run to second base and maybe even third." "The cheetah is very fast and might make it to third base," said Danny.

"Danny, it's important to always use two hands to catch the ball. Think of the ball as a slippery fish that wants to get back into the water. Danny imagined a fish headed towards his mitt. Speaking of things that live in the water, let's go see the octopus."

As they entered the building, Danny thought it would be wonderful to have eight arms like the octopus, especiall if he were playing baseball. He could throw a baseball, catch another, hit the ball, and even carry the equipme all at the same time!

"What a great zoo-ball day," said dad. Danny looked up and said, "Maybe next time we go to the zoo, we can get the animals to play a game of baseball!" Dad laughed and said, "You never know!" Danny climbed into bed, tired, but looking forward to the next day.

Illustrator's Bio:

As an art teacher for almost 30 years, I loved the challenge of creating the illustrations for this book. Baseball has a special place in my heart because my son played from the age of 9, all the way through college. I hope this story helps to inspire a greater understanding of baseball and a love for the sport.

Printed in the United States
Bookmasters